COPYRIGHT NOTICE:

ISBN #978-0-6151-9046-4 The following material has been copyrighted by Leah Young © 2008. All rights reserved. No part of this book may be reproduced in any form by any electronic or mechanical means (including photocopying, recording, or information storage and retrieval) without permission in writing from the publisher. For permissions address: The Dreamality Companies Publishing, books@dreamality.us.

Graphics by Mindy Sommers http://www.dreamingincolor.us

From the Author

*"What you see reflects your thinking.
And your thinking but reflects your choice of what you want to see."*
-- A Course In Miracles

In my life I practice seeing the reflection of the Divine expressing in me on my continuous journey to Enlightenment. I believe every thought is a prayer and affirmations support my choice to pray in a state of gratitude and knowing. It is my prayer that this collection of empowering truths be an expression of the divine flow in your life. Being the channel for each creative thought has brought me immeasurable joy. I know that practicing these affirmations consistently will result in an experience of joy "beyond the sky" for you as well.

I wish to take this opportunity to thank my family and friends for their continuing love and support. I am ever grateful for the presence of the Divine Flow in my life. Thank you, Mindy Sommers for creating the magnificent image which inspired and adorns this project.

Jesus the Nazarene said: "I declare a thing and it is done for me. My word accomplishes that which I send it out to do." I invite you to put your word to work for you in your life today.

I am one with the One.
The One is Me. I am the One.

Just as a cup of water from the ocean is the ocean
yet not the entire ocean, so too am I the Source.

I am accepting of what is.

I know that resistance is futile. As I love and accept with thanksgiving who and where I am now, I open the door to manifesting my highest good.

I am one with mankind.

*There is no beginning and no end
to the soul fabric from which we are woven.
I am what I see in others. It is good.*

I am the creator of my good.

I know that God is all there is. I am the One in the flesh and so I must bear responsibility for my choices.

I am happy.

I know that in preparing to be happy
I miss the opportunity to be happy.
I choose to be happy now.

I am detached.

*I release my attachment to the nature of the outcome,
knowing that whatever its character it is for my highest good.*

I am revealing myself.

I trust myself to be who I really am.
I trust others to receive who I really am with love.
I am free to be me.

I am in harmony with money.

I know that money is the out picturing of the Divine Source within. It is good to possess and circulate money.

I am empowered.

Powerlessness is trying to change that which I cannot.

Power is my ability to change that which I can.

I am empowered to know the difference.

I am complete.

*I know that I am made perfectly in the Image and Likeness of God.
I see myself whole and complete right now.*

I am feeling.

I release all judgment about my feelings. I am feeling whatever I am feeling right now. I observe my feelings as I observe the clouds in the sky. My feelings are and so am I.

I am free from all expectation.

Expectation is the mother of disappointment.
I know that all is as it should be.

I am magnificent.

I am a sculptor of the Divine able to carve out that which obscures the divine radiance at the core of my being.

I am One with the Source of my power.

*I recognize that the center of my being is Divine
and my power comes from this Source and no other.*

I am drawing the blueprint to my success.

Since I am connected to and am the channel for the Divine Infinite, I use my power to create a life of abundance, joy and happiness "beyond the sky".

I am living blissfully.

*I deserve a life overflowing with joy, happiness and abundance.
I live that life today and every day.*

I am loving myself deeply and extravagantly.

I am an attractive force in the world because I love myself unconditionally. I extend that love to all within my territory.

I am a radiant light.

I let my light shine in the world. Everything that I do and say is a reflection of the Divine that is within me.

I am alive to create.

*Everyday, every minute, every second
I am creating my reality. This is my purpose.*

I release fear and guilt.

*Instead today and everyday
I choose love and awareness for they bring life.*

I am plugged into inner peace.

I experience endless inner peace as I turn on and tune into the stillness of silence that is Spirit.

I am serene.

*I know that Divine Love is greater than any circumstance.
It is always available to me and mine.*

XXV

I am blessed.

I accept my good.
I am committed to pass on to others
the peace, hope, joy, and love within me.

XXVI

I am in prayer.

I open my heart to the infinite possibilities of the Divine for me and for you.
Peace, order and wellbeing are our experience now.

I am uplifted.

*The Grace of God uplifts me in every situation.
I surrender all concerns and open myself to Divine guidance.*

I am free.

The gift of Spirit expressing as freedom of thought, word and action, is mine at all times.

I am a Divine expression of healing love.

I express love as understanding and caring that strengthens me and my relationships.

xxx

I am adaptable.

I continue to expand my spiritual awareness and see the world from new perspectives, deepening my connection with the Divine and experiencing my highest good in all interactions.

I am an expression of Divine life.

I am created for life. I know the truth of who I am. My body is a temple of the Divine, my inheritance health and wholeness. I see the healing light of the Divine blessing and revitalizing me.

I am secure.

The Divine Spirit is ever present within me. I am confident and happy, feeling the love of God enfold me at all times. I know absolute peace.

I am in the Kingdom of God.

Here and now I experience Heaven. Forgiving love fills my heart, casting out all resentments. I receive joy, peace and abundance as my Divine gifts.

I am living in the present moment.

I open my life to my highest good by letting go of the past. The past has no power over me. I let go of any concerns for the future. I trust the Divine and embrace the now.

I am thankful.

I am filled with the joy of thanksgiving.
I am thankful for times of activity, rest and play.
I know the truth of who I am and I am glad.

I am a leader.

*Divinely inspired, I use my vision and creativity
for the good of myself and the world.*

XXXVII

I am courageous and strong.

I have all that I need to meet any circumstance. I respond to life's situations with grace, poise and wise action.
I am guided by my Divine connection.

I am expressing the Christ within.

Through the example of Jesus the Wayshower,
I am aware of my everlasting anointing.
I express the Christ presence in all my intentions and actions.

I Spirit.

I am all there is, ever was or ever shall be.
There is no beginning and no end.
I am.

I am brand new.

I am reborn with the dawning of each day,
I am free to choose anew.

I am well.

*I release all thoughts and feelings of disharmony and discord.
I rejoice in Spirit's healing design manifest in my life.
I am grateful for my health.*

I am emotionally balanced.

I am governed by Divine Power, Love & Mind.
I am centered and dynamically balanced.
I act according to my highest good at all times.

I am teachable.

I bless my mistakes as lessons learned and release them.
My heart is open and I respond to my Divine inner light.

I am Divine by design.

I am the greatest miracle of the universe expressing uniquely.
I release from consciousness al that contradicts who I really am.

I am meeting God in everyone.

I remind myself daily that God is in everyone.
I release all judgment and anger.
I express Divine love unconditionally.

I am forgiving.

I take back my power by forgiving.
I release myself and others from the prison of resentment.
I free myself to live in the eternal Now.
I acknowledge the Christ in you and me.

I am loving and lovable.

I love and accept myself.

I am safe.

I am at peace with life and the world that I live in.

I am the only one who thinks in my mind.

I am my own authority in my world.

I am already approved by God. I seek the approval of none other.

I am an independent thinker.

I am beyond group beliefs.
I am free from all external influence.
I let Spirit lead the way.

I am truly alive.

I flow with life.

I am centered in the joy and love of being alive.

I am enough.

I am divinely designed and therefore flawless.
I love me just the way I am.

I am expressing limitlessly.

I live free of others limiting ideas.
I am open to the possibilities.

I am alive in the Spirit.

I embrace my anointing as Spirit's vessel.
I live because It lives in me, as me and through me.

I am a free thinker.

I enjoy new and fun experiences with ease.

I am at peace.

I release the need to be right.

I am powerful and dynamic.

I am in charge of my mind and my life.
I accept my own divine power.

I am my own unique self.

I am creative.

I am special.

I am wonderful, wonderful me.

I am beautiful.

My beauty is self-defined.
I am unencumbered by media distortions
and popular culture.

I am the miracle.

I am God's most magnificent creation.
I am made in It's Image & Likeness.

I am free.

I alone am responsible for all that I do.
I alone am responsible for all that I am.

I am imagination.

I can achieve all that I can imagine.
Imagination is my direct connection to creation.

I am strong and courageous.

I am ready to realize my dreams fully.
No weapon formed against me shall prosper.

I am intelligent.

I know what I need to know at all times.
I open to the messages of the Divine Mind.

I am generous.

It is in the flow of giving that I receive all abundance.
I command all of the treasures of the Universe.

I am open to receive all of Life's riches.

*My blessings spill freely from the gates of heaven in my heart.
My wealth increases when I share it.*

I am a radiant light of God.

I let my light shine wherever I go.

LXVIII

I am good.

*If I recognize the sovereign power of God
then there can be none other.*

LXIX

I am healthy in all aspects of my being.

I control my well being.
My body is strong and vibrant.

I am always productive.

I am productive even when I am resting.
Rest rejuvenates my spirit and my body.

I am expressing Divine ideas.

I use the creative power of my imagination to give shape and form to Divine ideas. Divine intelligence + imagination = creation.

I am at one with the inner child within me.

I acknowledge that my inner child may still be suffering from old wounds.
I honor my inner child with compassion, love and protection.
Together we are unstoppable.

I am responsible for my own Spiritual Growth.

I shall not give away to anyone my power to think or to choose.

I know that God speaks to me the same as any who opens his heart to hear.

I am worthy.

I accept my Divine Birthright:
Happiness, Love, Peace, Well-Being

I am honest.

Whom shall I fear?
The truth is my freedom.
I live in it compassionately.

I am love.

The more I love the more love is returned to me.
God is Love.

I am grateful.

The joy of my gratitude is the seed that grows my abundance.

I am safe.

I release the armor of excess weight, pent up emotion, addiction, whatever I have hidden behind. The Power of God Protects me. I am free.

I am expressing in the Now.

I release the past. Let the dead bury the dead.

I am filled with Divine potential.

I commit to expressing my true nature in all that I do.

LXXXI

I am in tune with my inner voice.

I release all outer noise.
I embrace the warmth of Spirit's Voice.

I am sensual.

It is my sensuality that creates the wondrous experience of my surroundings. I celebrate and embrace my sense of touch, hearing, and feeling.

I am still.

Be still and know that I am God.
I know that I am in the right place at the right time.
I remain calm and at peace,
unaffected by whatever storms may rise around me.

LXXXIV

I am music.

I am in tune to the rhythm of my mind, body & soul.
Like the beat of the ancient drums, my heart beat sends me a message.
I listen.

I am awakened.

*I am committed to opening my eyes to a Spiritual vision.
I can see the infinite possibilities.*

I am complete.

I am one with my Source.

LXXXVII

I am obedient.

Spirit speaks to me through my inner voice.
When I listen and trust, all is well.

LXXXIX

xc

www.ingramcontent.com/pod-product-compliance
Lightning Source LLC
Chambersburg PA
CBHW041118300426
44112CB00002B/23